AF386236

With sincerest gratitude to Ann Eissinger
of the Puget Sound Nearshore Partnership
for her time and expertise.

And to heron watchers everywhere.

—BH

Text Copyright © 2026 Barbara Herkert
Illustration Copyright © 2026 Gordy Wright
Design Copyright © 2026 Tilbury House Publishers
Hardcover ISBN: 9781668955130

Library of Congress Cataloging-in-Publication Data
has been filed. LC record available at https://lccn.loc.gov/

Publisher expressly prohibits the use of this work in
connection with the development of any software program,
including, without limitation, training a machine learning
or generative artificial intelligence (AI) system.

All rights reserved. No part of this book may be reproduced
in any manner without the express written consent of the
publisher, except in the case of brief excerpts in critical
reviews and articles. All inquiries should be addressed to:

an imprint of
Cherry Lake Publishing Group
2395 South Huron Parkway, Suite 200
Ann Arbor, MI 48104

www.tilburyhouse.com

Printed and bound in the United States.

10 9 8 7 6 5 4 3 2 1

HERONRY

By Barbara Herkert

Art by Gordy Wright

TILBURY HOUSE PUBLISHERS

Spring dawns at the heronry.
The first bird arrives.
He lights with large, graceful wings,
long stilt-like legs.

Great Blue Herons are four feet tall and have a six-foot wingspan. They use their wings, trim legs, and strong toes for balance as they land on a variety of branches, thick and thin.

He chooses the best nest
near the top of the tallest tree.
With a bit of handiwork,
it will be as good as new.

Great Blue Herons often reuse their nests year after year. Males arrive first, collecting twigs to build up their chosen nests and attract females.

Misty morning at the heronry.
A female flies overhead.
The male bird flaps and flashes.
"Choose me! Choose me!"

Courtship is all about showing off elaborate feathers. Breeding Great Blue Herons grow long, narrow plumes on their heads, necks, and bodies.

More birds arrive.
Beaks clack, necks extend,
feathers flare.
All the tree's nests are occupied.
Count them—1, 2, 3, 4, 5!

Often, multiple pairs of herons nest in the same tall tree. The nests can be sixty to eighty feet above the ground. The pairs perform ritual displays by stretching, snapping, croaking, and clapping bill tips.

In the next tree over, and the next,
a multitude of stately silhouettes
perch above claimed nests
against a dusky sky.

Heronries range from a few to hundreds of nests. The birds stand over their nest, inspecting, making adjustments, adding twigs as needed or evergreen boughs along the edge. Nests can be three to four feet across and a foot deep.

Balmy afternoon at the heronry.
Females hunt in shallow
waters nearby.
Eat your fill!
Soon eggs will arrive.

Her long legs allow a Great Blue Heron to move slowly through the water without disturbing fish, and her sharp, pointed beak spears a meal. She will produce three to five eggs during the nesting season. Parents take turns incubating the eggs for approximately twenty-seven days.

Silver evening descends.
Males depart for the
hunting grounds.
What's on the menu?
Crabs, frogs, and fish!

Great Blue Herons stalk the coastlines of rivers, lakes, and streams mainly for fish, but they also eat crabs, frogs, salamanders, snakes, and small rodents.

Three chicks hatch, hungry for a meal.
They feed from Father's gullet full of fish.
Gronk! Mother lifts, long and limber.
Her turn to provide.

The parents take turns providing food for their young, fishing many times a day. The chicks will remain in the nest for up to sixty days before becoming full-grown fledglings.

Danger hovers at the heronry.
Dark shadows from above.
Father carefully covers his brood.
At last, the eagle moves on.

A Great Blue Heron's enemies are owls, eagles, and hawks. When an enemy raids the heronry, parent birds scream *Aawk!* in alarm. The alarm echoes through the heronry, alerting neighboring birds.

Squawk! Croak!
Mother counts her chicks—1, 2.
Of her three eggs,
two grow into strong nestlings.

Larger siblings often harass and even attack the smallest sibling. Owls, eagles, or hawks might fly off with a chick. Usually only two or three hatchlings survive per breeding pair.

The baby herons
flap their wings.
They squabble and
grasp beaks.
As they grow strong
and curious, they
venture to the nest below.

As they grow, young birds stand at the edge of the nest and exercise their muscles. When the nests are close together, larger, more adventurous chicks will gather in their neighbor's nest to investigate.

Nearly grown at the heronry.
The chicks look much like their parents now.
They preen their feathers,
then face the wind for their first flight.

A daily routine of preening makes sure that each feather is in good condition and in its proper place for flying. Preening can last up to twenty minutes. Fledglings face into the wind for lift-off. Their first flight is short, usually to the nearest tree.

With arched wings and curved necks,
the fledglings land at the hunting grounds.
Their pointed bills are poised
and ready for a fishy meal.

When in flight, Great Blue Herons stretch their long legs behind them and draw their necks into an "S" shape. Young birds gradually take longer flights and follow adult birds to foraging sites.

Nest by nest, the heronry scatters.
Whomp! Whomp!
Powerful wing strokes fill the sky.
Some birds stay close, some travel far.

During the non-breeding season, herons leave their colonies for shorelines, marshes, and farmlands. They find shelter behind thickets or in trees, where they preen or sleep.

Quiet falls at the heronry.
The nests sit empty now.
Next spring, the herons will return,
performing nature's dance once more.

After only three months, young herons must fend for themselves. Fledglings may group together over the first winter. Adults return to their mostly solitary lives until the following spring when they gather at the heronry again.

More Facts About Great Blue Herons

GREAT BLUE HERONS are the largest members of the heron family, at nearly four feet tall. With their tall, twiggy legs and long, curved necks, they are a combination of awkwardness and elegance, bizarreness and beauty. Great Blues are common in many parts of the United States. Many migrate to warmer climates during the winter months, while those in more temperate climates may stay year-round.

Great Blue Herons are non-dimorphic, meaning males and females look the same, with no size difference between the sexes. They share in the raising of their young and can live for fifteen to twenty years. They breed just once a year.

Between the 1870s and the mid-1920s, tens of millions of Great Blue Herons were killed for their feathers to adorn women's hats. Hunters targeted heronries—the large colonies where they nest—killing parent birds and leaving the young to die. Fortunately, Great Blue Herons are now protected by federal law, but maintaining their habitats is crucial to their survival. This includes healthy waterways for food and adequate trees for nesting.

Heronries must be protected and restored by reducing pollution and limiting development in these areas. Most herons are sensitive to the presence of humans and may abandon their eggs if frightened. During nesting season, human activity around heronries should be buffered by barriers such as fences.

Few animals symbolize conservation as beautifully as the Great Blue Heron. It resides on the shores, beaches, streams, rivers, marshes, grasslands, and forests of our world. Protecting the heron and its habitat helps protect the environment we all share. You can help by joining a heron stewardship program in your area or volunteering to maintain and monitor nesting sites. When you view a heronry or witness a Great Blue Heron calmly walking along the shore, you will understand that these stately birds must always be with us.

For more information about preserving heron habitat, check out the heron conservation programs in your state or contact the following agencies: The Nature Conservancy, the U.S. Environmental Protection Agency, the U.S. Army Corps of Engineers, and the U.S. Fish and Wildlife Service.

BIBLIOGRAPHY

Butler, Robert W. *The Great Blue Heron.* UBC Press, 1997.

Eissinger, Ann. "Great Blue Herons in Puget Sound."
Puget Sound Nearshore Partnership,
Technical Report 2006–2007. Seattle District,
U.S. Army Corps Of Engineers, Seattle, Washington.

Mock, Douglas W. "Pair-Formations Diplays of the
Great Blue Heron." *The Wilson Bulletin,* Vol. 88,
No. 2, June 1976, pp. 185–376.

Simpson, Bud with Foreword by Paul Knoop.
Nature's Way: The Great Blue Heron. Biblio Publishing, 2016.

Strattin, Lisa. *Facts About the Great Blue Heron:
A Picture Book for Kids.* Create Space Independent
Publishing Platform, 2016.

Tekiela, Stan. *Cranes, Herons & Egrets.*
Adventure Publications, 2016.

Map courtesy of Cephas, CC BY-SA 4.0,
via Wikimedia Commons. Colors and shapes
have been retouched for use in print.